EAT
MOVE
BE STILL

LISA COX

BALBOA.PRESS
A DIVISION OF HAY HOUSE

Balboa Press books may be ordered through booksellers or by contacting:

Balboa Press
A Division of Hay House
1663 Liberty Drive
Bloomington, IN 47403
www.balboapress.com
844-682-1282

Print information available on the last page.

ISBN: 978-1-9822-5165-9 (sc)
ISBN: 978-1-9822-5152-9 (e)

Balboa Press rev. date: 09/04/2020

Hello and welcome!

Here are some simple, easy suggestions to help you on your way or encourage you to stay a healthy vibrant being on this planet. Read it all the way through if you'd like and then use it daily to add variety to your routine.

Listen to YOUR body. Get to know YOURSELF. If something hurts physically, don't do it...if something hurts emotionally, lean into it and do some writing about it...We are on a journey and we are in this together. You are not alone...☺

EAT

Stay on the perimeter of
the grocery store.
It's where the foods with the simplest
ingredients are, except the bakery...☺

MOVE

REMEMBER SOMETHING...

YOU ARE WONDERFUL
WORTHY
IMPORTANT
AND FABULOUS!

GO BE YOURSELF TODAY!

BE STILL

Insight... Looking within to find your
answers... asking that place inside
of you that knows the answer.
If you don't know that place, take some
quiet time to introduce yourself to that
place...sit and close your eyes, allow
your thoughts to pass on by, come
back to the center and breathe.
Practice this every day for 1 week.

EAT

Some days you just want to eat things
that just aren't that great for you.
It's not the end of the world, just do
it with the full awareness that you're
doing it! ENJOY EVERY BITE!
You might find that you don't
need to go as 'crazy' as if you
weren't paying attention!

MOVE

Interval training is one of the most
efficient ways to burn calories and
change body composition.
Pick 3 exercises to do -
Do each one for 30 seconds for
a total of 5 minutes, about 4 sets
Example – Jumping Jacks 30 seconds
Lunges 30 seconds
Bicep curls 30 seconds
Repeat
Walk around the block briskly –
Done!

BE STILL

Healing happens when I address and
honor what I am experiencing.
Am I ...
anxious?
In physical pain?
Unsafe?
Feeling addicted to something?
Fearful?
Sad?
Angry?
Worried?
Resentful?
Avoiding something?
Shameful?
Write about it, call a friend.
TAKE ACTION

EAT

When it seems as though you've tried everything and you just keep returning to your same old habits, but you really DO want to eat healthier...STOP. Start journaling. Putting your struggles down on paper can help you release the broken record of bad habits. Communicate with yourself, call a friend, more will be revealed.

MOVE

Do an inventory of your workout clothes.

-Are your shoes worn and
ready to be replaced?

-Is it time for a new shirt?
-Pair of shorts?
-Sports bra?

You're worth it!:)

BE STILL

When I face my 'demons'
it allows me to feel...
Peace
Calm
Joy
Happy
Present
Loved
Curious
Open
Willing
Held
Connected
Possibility
Hope
Courageous
Let healing happen

EAT

If you can't pronounce the ingredients,
it's probably best to pass...

MOVE

From this day forward...

I WILL COMMIT TO BE FIT!

What does that look like?

A commitment to walking four 20 minute
sessions per week is a great start!

YOU CAN DO IT!

BE STILL

An exercise...
I CAN'T
I WON'T
I HATE
I CAN'T
I WON'T
How does your body feel when
you declare these words? Sit
with that for just a moment...
Now...
I CAN!
I WILL!
I LOVE!
I CAN!
I WILL!
How does your body feel when you
say these words? Sit with that for
just a moment...How do you feel?
What do you choose?

EAT

Each day is an opportunity to express
love for ourselves by putting wholesome,
simple foods into our body.
Make today a day that reflects care
and concern for your health. Eat foods
that show the commitment to health
that you want to confirm for yourself.
Choose simple, fresh ingredients,
lots of fresh water.
You're worth the effort! ☺

MOVE

Standing upright, shoulders down,
Stretch your arms above your
head...Gently and slowly point
your fingertips to the sky,
s-t-r-e-t-c-h your shoulders
slowly up and release...
Bring your fingertips towards your toes...
And release...

Do this 3 times today ☺

BE STILL

Fulfillment is a state of mind.
It can be felt figuratively or actually.
By recognizing fulfillment as a 'feeling'
one just has to access the feeling
and experience being fulfilled. This
is contrary to only feeling fulfilled if
certain things are 'in place' in our lives.
Contemplate what makes
you feel 'fulfilled'.
Can you actualize that feeling right now?
If not, why not...
What would make you feel
fulfilled right now...
Is this a goal you would like to achieve...
or can you look at the fact that all
you have to do is create the feeling
of being fulfilled in your mind...

EAT

Moderation
Always a great practice when
approaching a food plan.
Being mindful when it comes to
food creates a space of awareness
and centeredness; always helpful in
making the best choice for health.

MOVE

Pick a drawer to clean out today!
(Yes! A drawer!)

Sometimes we feel stuck...
Am I... In a worn out pattern? In a
funk? In a negative thought?...
Organizing something, even the smallest
area, can bring forward positive motion
that starts the process flowing again.

Try it!

BE STILL

Learning about who you are is a practice.
Just like anything you want to be good
at, you need to practice the act of
self-reflection.

-Commit to Sit-

Reflect on your hopes and
dreams for your life...
Visualize what you would like
to manifest for yourself

EAT

You are what you eat –
Fruits, vegetables, whole grains,
lots of fresh water...
Sugar, processed food, salt...
Do an experiment...try eating as close
as you can to nothing processed for a
week and see how you feel...how much
energy you have, how your attitude
improves, how much better you sleep...

Move

Walk instead of drive to an
appointment today...

Your attitude will improve
one step at a time!

BE STILL

Take the time to connect to the "stillness'.
A quiet, unknown place has benefits that
can only be described and understood
by the people who do it. Allow yourself
to explore this unknown corner of
consciousness that so few dare to go...
The benefits are wonderful.
Peace of mind, a sense of calm,
less reactive, more willing...

EAT

Positive, loving thoughts can help you
make good food choices. Our body wants
to comply and move towards wholesome
choices when the thoughts we send
it are joyful and encouraging. Like -
I am worth treating my body with love.
I am excited to eat clean, healthy foods.
I love the person I am becoming.
Just to name a few <3

MOVE

Moving mindfully brings us
into the right now.

Bring attention to your body.
How do you feel right now?
Notice the areas that are calling
your attention...breathe and
allow the communication...

BE STILL

Commit to one week of 5 minutes
of self-reflection each day.
Focus on a word, a phrase or a flower...
Allow all other thoughts to pass
by... Watch your life expand...

EAT

Emotional eating can seem to 'satisfy'
for a moment, only to be left with the
regret and remorse of consuming a large
amount of calories with no 'reward'.
Often, an emotional eating session is
an attempt to ground oneself...a way to
come back into your body...instead of
using food for that...try writing about your
feelings...listen to some soothing music or
go for a walk...The outcome is much more
rewarding...It might leave you feeling more
centered and grounded without regret <3

MOVE

Just Do It!

20 minutes a day of sustained movement...

It does a body good!

BE STILL

Inspirational readings can
ignite the fire in your soul.
Reading books from others that have gone
before us on this path of self reflection
encourages us to have a healthy
attitude and approach to life that
can guide our wellness path.
Some wonderful authors are Pema
Chodron, Eckhart Tolle and Louise Hay.

EAT

Everyone has different ways that work for them when it comes to eating. However, if it isn't working for you, why don't you try something different? Being open and willing to change is hard but you can do it! Try something new TODAY. Break that old pattern TODAY...see what change it brings...you are being supported!

MOVE

Try this –

15 Jumping Jacks
5 Push Ups
10 Windmills
Do all one time through
3 times this week!
Physical and mental agility
help your mood!

BE STILL

No one has your circumstances. Even
your siblings have a different perspective
of what goes on in your family.
Honor the fact that you are on this planet,
in this body for a particular reason.
Honor the fact that you are exactly
where you are supposed to be.
Good or bad, right or wrong.
Allow time to honor your journey.
Sit for a moment and quietly
reflect on how far you've come.
Allow some time to just BE.

EAT

Plan your meals today!
Lots of fresh veggies and fruits
Fresh clean water
Lean protein and whole grains
What will you choose today?
How does that make you feel?

MOVE

Try this –

March in place!
Pump your arms!

Count to 50

Repeat 3 x's

BE STILL

Taking the time to quiet our minds
is a gift that we can give ourselves.
When nothing seems to give relief,
try listening to the silence...it has
a beautiful message of peace

EAT

Mindful food choices can be a wonderful first step to move towards good health. Choosing simple things to eat with few ingredients is the best way to make preparing food something you enjoy. Fruit, nuts, vegetables, lean meat, fish, rice, potatoes...just to name a few.

Keep it simple...

MOVE

Stand upright with room to spread your
arms and legs wider than your shoulders.
Hold your arms out and gently, slowly
touch your right knee with your left hand
or touch your toes, now switch sides...
Do this 10 times, mindfully, on
each side...feel the stretch, feel
the mind/body connection...

BE STILL

It is just as important to rest as it is to move daily. The simplest way to connect with oneself is to take the time to be quiet and connect with the inner wellspring of passion, compassion and joy. When I connect to my inner place of joy, I am free to experience joy on the outside. A simple practice...

EAT

When was the last time you
ate something green?
5 servings of vegetables per day is a
wonderful way to keep the DR. away ☺
Some good solid choices are
Spinach
Broccoli
Kale
Zucchini
Chard
Just to name a few... commit to
at least 3 servings of the good
stuff 5 days per week!
Google your favorite recipes
and get creative!

MOVE

Getting out in the fresh air and pulling
weeds or planting a plant, flowers or some
tomatoes can be a rewarding activity.

Getting your hands in the dirt
is good for the soul. ☺

BE STILL

Sometimes what we can visualize for ourselves is just a fraction of what is possible. Take a few moments to just stand there and visualize being open enough to receive more than you can even imagine...Open your heart to the possibility that you are worthy of all things good...visualize yourself receiving wonderful gifts of peace.

EAT

Think of food as energy. Choose
foods that are simple and
clean to fill the 'furnace'
with clean burning fuel.
Lean protein, fresh vegetables
and fruits and whole grains.
These simple ingredients are a very
important part of the healthy choices
that help drive us towards being the
best person we can be each day.

Today I will be mindful of my
choices and love myself with
clean, simple ingredient foods.

MOVE

Tomorrow is a great day to start.
Today is even better!
Get some shoes on and go outside!
Walk around the block, walk to
the store, walk to the park.
You will be amazed at the fresh
perspective it will offer!

BE STILL

Self-reflection is such an important
tool to help you feel grounded. Taking
the time to go over your day, see
where you might need to apologize
or check if you need to do something
to right a wrong, or just pat yourself
on the back for a day well lived. ☺

EAT

You're really hungry. You are out
and about and you know you
have to have something...
Good simple choices from a convenience
store...small container of trail mix or nuts,
Piece of fresh fruit,
A small pack of cheese chunks,
A granola bar...
Usually when hunger has gone too far
we want to grab candy...it will curb
your hunger but your mood will come
crashing down soon after...when in
doubt, play it out in your mind...it
often feels better to eat 'cleaner'...

MOVE

If your natural tendency is NOT to move,
try setting out your clothes for a brisk
morning walk/jog the night before.

It sets the intention and commitment to
connect with the earth AND your body.

Always a positive step towards
a healthy lifestyle!

BE STILL

Guided meditations are a wonderful
way to start a meditation practice.
By choosing a specific thing you'd like
to focus on; breath, connecting with the
angels, chakra clearing, ect. Google it!
There is a guided meditation for
almost anything you'd like...

EAT

Sometimes you get in a food rut...
especially when you aren't a person
who likes to cook...Get creative, try
something you've never eaten before!
You might be pleasantly surprised!

MOVE

Different seasons call for
different ways to move.
Winter is more challenging to be
outside, but can be invigorating!
Sometimes 'moving' in the winter can
consist of 20 minutes of some yoga
stretches and sometimes it can consist
of an entire day on the slopes.
There are so many ways to connect
your mind to your body.
What will you do today?

BE STILL

Negative thinking can be just as 'toxic'
as unhealthy food choices and can even
draw you towards unhealthy food. Stay
mindful of your thinking today...each
time you have a negative thought,
Think of a positive thought...
Create a habit of positive self talk...

EAT

Soups are a fantastic way to get
vegetables into your body.
Throwing a homemade soup
together is easy!
1 medium onion - chopped
2 cloves garlic - chopped
5 carrots - chopped
3 celery stalks - chopped
Zucchini - chopped
1 can kidney or cannellini beans
1 can of seasoned tomatoes
64 ounces of vegetable or chicken broth
1tsp oregano, 1tsp basil, 1tsp thyme,
2 TBS salt or dried bouillon
In a large saucepan, sauté first 5
ingredients for 10-15 minutes, until
softer add broth and beans, spices and
bouillon simmer for 30 minutes - Enjoy!

MOVE

When was the last time you skipped? ☺

Skipping is usually only done by
children...there is something so
playful in skipping...Try it!
If you really cannot physically do it, close
your eyes and visualize yourself skipping...
visualize yourself skipping and laughing
and happy and free...a good reminder...

BE STILL

There are so many distractions in life
that pull us away from the peace and
quiet of getting to know our truest self.
The gift that you can give yourself each
day is a quiet moment to just be.
Breathe in and out...honor
the space that is you.

Sit quietly for 10 minutes...just BE...
☺

EAT

Protein and how much you should have
can vary from person to person...
A good way to determine how much
protein you need per meal is in the
palm of your hand...literally!
The palm of your personal hand is a good
and perfect size of how much protein
you personally can eat at each meal. Add
a bunch of veggies to that and enjoy!

MOVE

Sometimes the only thing that is holding us back is our thoughts.

Go beyond your limited thought and take action on something you've wanted to do for a long time...YOU CAN DO IT!

BE STILL

In our attempt to be productive
members of society,
we do and do, go and go without pause.
Sometimes the pause allows
us to step back
and acknowledge all we have done.
A chance to allow ourselves to reset.
The pause is actually just as
important as the forward motion.
Take time to pause and reflect today.
Notice where you may need to adjust,
notice where you've done a great job and
acknowledge yourself for that!

EAT

An energizing smoothie is a good
way to add fruits and vegetables
into your daily routine.
Berries, spinach, banana, kale, almond
milk, orange juice, almond butter, mango,
get creative...a simple blender can be
a great investment for your health!

MOVE

Small goals can lead to BIG changes...
start with a small goal to move for even
5 minutes today...sustained movement
directed towards a healthy heart
and mind...YOU ARE WORTH IT!

BE STILL

Progress Not Perfection
Perfectly Imperfect
Enjoy the Journey
All you have is NOW
Be Still And Know...

EAT

Caffeine is a tricky substance.
Too much can wreak havoc
on our systems,
Many of us have succumbed to its grip.
As with most things we put in our bodies,
moderation is always the key.
When we make our health our top
priority, we naturally are able to mindfully
recognize how much is too much.
Notice how you feel when you put
things in your body and listen to those
prompts that caution you...they're
very quiet and quite empowering!

MOVE

When doing an interval circuit workout, let one of the stations be a rest station... You'll be amazed how much energy you have for the next dynamic move with complete rest for the duration of the timed station... In life, rest is just as important as moving. Balance is such an important component to a healthy life. Take an inventory of how balanced your life is...stepping back and taking stock can re-center your intentions to be the best you!

BE STILL

Our ego can limit us in so many ways...
telling us what we can and can't do
Set the ego aside for a moment
and close your eyes.
Let yourself imagine something
that you would love to do.
Let your imagination go with it.
Visualize the possibility of that very
thing happening...coming true.
Write it down.
Go for it!
What you believe you can achieve!

EAT

Simple
Vs.
Convenient

Simple, healthy food choices are low ingredient foods without a 'package'. Convenience foods are full of preservatives, large amounts of salt and many ingredients that are not recommended to ingest on a daily basis. Yes, they taste wonderful and the best way to incorporate them in your food plan is occasionally...

71

MOVE

Remember, your life is more important
than what other people think of you.
If you are not walking outside because
you are worried that you don't 'look' good
enough, here to tell you that YOU ARE
PERFECT JUST THE WAY YOU ARE.
Your health is so much more important
than what you look like, start today,
Move your body!

BE STILL

Starting each day with a fresh
perspective is always important. No
matter what happened yesterday, today
is a new day with new possibilities.
Take a deep breath, give yourself an
encouraging pause to remind yourself who
you are, why you matter and what your
purpose is for today...you don't know?
Take some time to reflect on those
things...start a journal...it's important
to know yourself and who you truly are
without any outside influences...it makes it
a lot easier to know where you're going ;)

EAT

Fresh fruit isn't always available.
Frozen fruit is a great alternative; just
check that there is no added sugar.
Simple is best...

MOVE

Let's face it...abdominal work
might not be your favorite...but...
have you tried standing abs?
Standing abdominal work can be fun!
Stand up nice and straight, pull
your leg up diagonally across your
body, then the other leg, chest up...
head forward...Start with 10 on each
side...get that heart pumpin'!

Google Standing Abs and
strengthen that core of yours!

It's your point of power!

BE STILL

Taking the time to connect to the 'stillness', that quiet, 'unknown' place has benefits that can only be described and understood by the people who actually attempt it. Allow yourself to explore this unknown corner of consciousness that so few dare to go...the benefits are wonderful!

EAT

It seems that over the years society
has leaned towards more is better.
Bigger portions, bigger sizes of
drinks, more of everything!
When it comes to food, more and
bigger is not necessarily better.
Too much of anything tends
to spill out the sides...
Focus on moderation of all things you put
in your mouth today...notice where the
excess is not necessarily the right choice...
Be mindful and listen to your body...
An important practice for a balanced life<3

MOVE

They say there are 2 things in life you
can count on...Death and taxes...
OK...yes...
Now get on your workout shoes and
get outside...walk, run, skip, smile...
It does a body good ;)

BE STILL

Learning about who you are is a
practice. Just like anything you
want to be good at, you need to
practice the art of self reflection.
It is a commitment to a better you, a
commitment to getting to know yourself
by allowing the thoughts from your soul
to fill the empty space you leave for it.
Sit, be quiet, reflect...
Commit to sit<3

EAT

A path near a creek is often a wonderful
place to discover a blackberry patch.
Harvest time in the Northern
Hemisphere is in the summer.
Find a path near you and explore
where you might find some berry
bushes...Watch for the stickers!
A beautiful walk in nature
with a sweet treat...
Can't find any? The treat is being
outside...notice the birds and the sky...
A wonderful gift...

MOVE

Don't feel like exercising?

DO IT ANYWAY

You won't regret it!

BE STILL

It has been found that practicing
compassion is actually anti-inflammatory.
Observing animals, petting an
animal, watching birds, reflecting
on love for another...take the time
to do this and practice peace.

EAT

Spices are a wonderful way
to enhance food.
The spice world is waiting for you...
Get creative! Try a new recipe with a
spice you've never tried before...
What's your favorite spice?

MOVE

Supermans!
Superwomans!
Superhumans!

Lay on the floor face down
Arms in front of your head
Gently lift your arms and legs up,
just a little so your torso is the
only thing touching the floor
Lay arms and legs back down
Lift up again and then down
Repeat 5 – 10 times
Slowly get up off that floor
Good Job!

BE STILL

When the stress of the outside
world and all its worries and
fears feel like too much...
Know there is a place you can
go where it is alright...
A beautiful instrumental song to
bring your mind peace...to help you
drop out of the frenzy and into the
peace...or even just a quiet room
where you won't be disturbed. Take
the time...5 minutes, 10 minutes.
Feel the message that your body has
for you...Listen with reverence...<3

EAT

Who says you can't have
dinner for breakfast?
Who says you can't have
breakfast for dinner!?
Change it up!
Sometimes we just get bored
with the same routine...
Creative changes that 'wake us up' to
something different and new can help
our mood and bring back the fun in life!
Simple suggestions...<3

MOVE

We eat for energy. We move
to release that energy. Our
bodies are made to move.
Different personalities have different
needs when it comes to movement.
Getting to know what works for you
personally is part of the fun!
There are so many ways to move our cells
around so they regenerate and continue
to stay (or become) strong and healthy...

BE STILL

There are 7 Chakras that
we hold in our body.
Chakras are the life force within...
The Base Chakra
The Sacral Chakra
The Solar Plexus Chakra
The Heart Chakra
The Throat Chakra
The Third Eye Chakra
The Crown Chakra
Our essence is created from these
intuitive points in our bodies...
Being still and honoring these points
is a wonderful way to connect to
our purpose and our power...<3

I hope you have enjoyed some simple
suggestions to help you navigate
this crazy thing we call life.

The intention of this book is to remind
you that having a positive attitude towards
your health is far more empowering
than fearing that you will get sick.
Mind, Body and Soul
There is only one you.
You deserve the best life you can imagine!

Focus on being strong and healthy
and that's what you'll get!

Always look at what you are grateful for!
It will bring you peace inside...

Printed in the United States
By Bookmasters